LITERACY LINE-UP

POETRY PATTERNS

COMPILED BY FIONA WATERS

CONTENTS

NS	2	Riddles	16
S	2	Nonsense	18
S	5		
	6	**SOUND AND**	
S	8	**PERFORMANCE POEMS**	19
	9		
	10	**PROSE AND**	
	11	**SHAPE POEMS**	**23**
		Prose	23
	12	Epitaphs	27
S	12	Shape	28
	14		

PATTERNS

COUPLETS

The Walrus

The walrus lives on icy floes
And unsuspecting Eskimoes.

Don't bring your wife to Arctic Tundra
A Walrus may bob up from undra.

Michael Flanders

On the vanity of earthly greatness

The tusks that clashed in mighty brawls
Of mastodons, are billiard balls.

The sword of Charlemagne the Just
Is ferric oxide, known as rust.

The grizzly bear whose potent hug
Was feared by all, is now a rug.

Great Caesar's bust is on the shelf,
And I don't feel so well myself!

Arthur Guiterman

Catch

There once was a fisherman of Scrabster
Caught in his pot a gey queer lapster.

Thought he, this lapster's a sure sellar
A tail it has, and a wee propellor,

In fact, it's no ordinary lapster felly,
It looks far more like a peedie heli-

You know yon kind of hoverlapster,
A what do you call it, helicapster.

Aye, aye, it's a peedie helicapster:
There's lots are caught in the sea off Scrabster.

Ian Hamilton Finlay

LIMERICKS

An architect sat back and laughed:
'I know that my new plans seem daft.
On each of the floors,
There's no windows or doors –
But at least I've got rid of the draught.'

Frank Richards

A young girl who was fond of meringue,
Let thoughts of her figure go hingue;
She ate them in tons,
Along with cream buns,
Until she went off with a bingue.

Val Pöhler

SONNETS

The Skylight

You were the one for skylights. I opposed
Cutting into the seasoned tongue-and-groove
Of pitch pine. I liked it low and closed,
Its claustrophobic, nest-up-on-the-roof
Effect. I liked the snuff-dry feeling.
The perfect, trunk-lid fit of the old ceiling.
Under there, it was all hutch and hatch.
The blue slates kept the heat like midnight thatch.

But when the slates came off, extravagant
Sky entered and held surprise wide open.
For days I felt like an inhabitant
Of that house where the man sick of the palsy
Was lowered through the roof, had his sins forgiven,
Was healed, took up his bed and walked away.

Seamus Heaney

Sonnet LV

Not marble, nor the gilded monuments
Of princes, shall outlive this powerful rime;
But you shall shine more bright in these contents,
Than unswept stone, besmear'd with sluttish time.
When wasteful war shall statues overturn,
And broils root out the work of masonry,
Nor Mars his sword nor war's quick fire shall burn
The living record of your memory.
'Gainst death and all-oblivious enmity
Shall you pace forth; your praise shall still find room
Even in the eyes of all posterity,
That wear this world out to the ending doom.
So, till the judgement that yourself arise,
You live in this, and dwell in lovers' eyes.

William Shakespeare

CINQUAINS

Scarlet
geranium
the felt pens of your buds
are busting to splash summer on
my sill

Geoffrey Holloway

November Night

Listen . . .
With faint dry sound,
Like steps of passing ghosts,
The leaves, frost-crisped, break from the trees
And fall.

Adelaide Crapsey

HAIKU

Just a green olive
In its own little egg-cup:
It can feed the sky

Kit Wright

                morning exercise –
          blackbird on the lawn
       stretches a worm

Jackie Hardy

A bitter morning

A bitter morning,
sparrows sitting together
without any necks.

Anonymous
Translated from Japanese by J. W. Hackett

Like a boomerang,
mean words behind your friend's back
can come back to you.

Mike Jubb

Highcoo

Up on the ledges
Above the city traffic:
Fond sounds of pigeons.

Eric Finney

TANKA

A tanka

wallows in the high
waves and rising winds, like a
long stick in a stream:
when it cracks thousands of birds
and fish will float like dead leaves.

Dave Calder

Acrostics

December

W ater
I ces
N aked
T rees;
E arth
R ests.

Judith Nicholls

Yeti

You
Enormous
Tibetan
Iceman

Gervase Phinn

An Acrostic

A favourite literary devi
Ce is the one whe
Re the first letter
Of each line spell
S out the subject the poe
T wishes to write about.
I must admit, I
Can't see the point myself.

Roger McGough

IMAGES

MINIATURES

Shadows

Pictures
painted
by
the
sun

rubbed
out
by
the
clouds

Gary Boswell

Ten Syllables for Spring

daffylonglegs
blowing
buttered trumpets.

Sue Cowling

The Dog

The truth I do not stretch or shove
When I state the dog is full of love.
I've also proved, by actual test,
A wet dog is the lovingest.

Ogden Nash

The Fairy Ring

Here the horse-mushrooms make a fairy ring,
    Some standing upright and some overthrown,
A small Stonehenge, where heavy black slugs cling
    And bite away, like Time, the tender stone.

Andrew Young

Kennings

SHH!

Silent moon flyer
On man's murdered hedge
Catches sounds
Of its furry food

*(Barn owl on a fence listens for
mice and voles)*

Ian Larmont

Winter Ocean

Many-maned scud-thumper, tub
of male whales, maker of worn wood, shrub-
ruster, sky-mocker, rave!
portly pusher of waves, wind-slave.

John Updike

River

boat-carrier
bank-lapper
home-provider
tree-reflector
leaf-catcher
field-wanderer
stone-smoother
fast-mover
gentle-stroller
sun-sparkler
sea-seeker

June Crebbin

RIDDLES

Hodmandod Riddle

Though not a cow
I have horns;
Though not an ass
I carry a pack-saddle;
And wherever I go
I leave silver behind me.

Traditional   *(Snail)*

I go through the wood in silence
and come out on to the snow
where I leave my prints
though I have no footsteps,
where I speak your heart
though I cannot breathe.

Kit Wright   *(Pencil lead)*

Over the water,
And under the water,
And always with its head down!

In rainy squall or pattering shower,
I open like a sudden flower;
But when the wind blows strong to gale,
I huddle close and furl my sail;
Then, peg-leg hopping down the street,
I follow close my master's feet.

John Cunliffe

(Umbrella)

NONSENSE

One fine October morning
In September, last July,
The moon lay thick upon the ground,
The snow shone in the sky;
The flowers were singing gaily
And the birds were in full bloom,
I went down to the cellar
To sweep the upstair room.

Anonymous

My Garden

I went down the garden, and what should I see
But an elephant's nest in a rhubarb tree;
And as I came in with an elephant's egg
I stepped on a snake which had only one leg.
But when the sun rose at the end of the day,
The snake and the elephant both flew away.

Roger Lancelyn Green

SOUND AND PERFORMANCE POEMS

Get Off This Estate

'Get off this estate.'
'What for?'
'Because it's mine.'
'Where did you get it?'
'From my father.'
'Where did he get it?'
'From his father.'
'And where did he get it?'
'He fought for it.'
'Well, I'll fight you for it.'

Carl Sandburg

Rap Connected

We were born to rap
We were born to dance
We were born to sing
We are Queens an Kings
We were born to live de life dat we luv
We were born to luv de life dat we live,
We were born to twist

We were born to shout
We can keep it in
We can hang it out
We got riddim in us mate

Get infected,
Shout it loud
We are connected.

We were born to share
An hav fun whilst here,
So if you don't care
Go somewhere you square,
If you are aware
You will be respected
We all share the air and

We are black an brown
We are white an sound
We have pride of place
We are on de case
We are wild an tame
We are all de same

Sister, brother, kid,
We are connected.

Benjamin Zephaniah

Kalahari Days Hot

Kalahari days hot,
Kalahari days cold,
Baby in a kaross cape
Nine days old.
Block out the desert heat,
Keep out the desert cold
Baby in a kaross cape
Nine days old.

Virginia Kroll

Unemployable

'I usth thu workth in the thircusth,'
He said,
Between the intermittent showers that
emerged from his mouth.
'Oh,' I said, 'what did you do?'
'I usth thu catcth bulleth in my theeth.'

Gareth Owen

PROSE AND
SHAPE POEMS

PROSE

Painter's Diary

MONDAY: Painted the town RED. All
               benches wet!

TUESDAY: Boring sunset – added a dash
               of ORANGE.

WEDNESDAY: Rollered the desert YELLOW.
               Miles and miles of it!

THURSDAY: Tried out different shades
               of GREEN on trees etc.

FRIDAY: Colour-washed the sky
               BLUE – a bit streaky.

SATURDAY: Daubed the evening INDIGO.
               Deeply satisfying.

SUNDAY: Tidied paintbox.

N.B.   Need more VIOLET
               new brush
               sketch pad
               pencils

Sue Cowling

Mars to Earth

MARS, THE GOD OF WAR
TO EARTH, MEN OF PEACE.

MARS   HELLO, THIS IS MARS. CAN
YOU HEAR ME, EARTH?

EARTH   yes, we can hear you. Speak to us.

MARS   I WISH TO SPEAK TO THE
MEN OF PEACE.

EARTH   we are those people. Speak
in truth.

MARS   NO, NOT TO THE LEADERS
OF THE WORLD.

EARTH   but we are the GREATEST OF
ALL MANKIND.

MARS   NO, I WOULD SPEAK TO
THE meekest minds.

EARTH   THEY'RE NOT IMPORTANT.
YOU WOULDN'T BE HEARD

MARS   I will not talk to the ones
who shout.

EARTH   BUT WE ARE THE ONES
WHO WIN ALL WARS.

MARS   You are the ones who'll destroy
            the stars.

EARTH WHAT ON EARTH IS THIS
            TALK ABOUT?

MARS   War and peace. I will speak
            no more.

EARTH SPEAK UP, MARS. YOUR
            SIGNAL'S LOST. WE'VE
            LOST ALL CONTACT.
            MARS IS A GHOST.

we're the children of earth, mars. whisper.
we hear.

Berlie Doherty

MISSING

MISSING

HAVE YOU SEEN THIS DOT?

small black answers to

Dot or Full Stop

Disappeared last Friday

Dotnapped?

? and ' both pining

e mail desperate

contact KEYBOARD WATCH

to earn cash reward

Epitaphs

In the graveyard of Malmesbury Abbey is the headstone of Hannah Twynnoy who was attacked by a tiger which had escaped from a travelling circus:

In bloom of Life
She's snatched from hence,
She had not room
To make defence;
For Tyger fierce
Took Life away,
And here she lies
In a bed of clay
Until the Resurrection Day.

Poor John lies buried here;
Although he was both hale and stout,
Death stretched him on the bitter bier,
In another world he hops about.

SHAPE

Africa

```
                    THE SONG
             THE BURNING SONG
           THE DEMON VULTURES
         THE HAZY TENTS  THE RAW
      HORIZONS  THE DRUGGED SANDS  THE SCREAMING
    THUNDER  THE RATTLING BONES  THE DUSTY MOUTHS
   THE INFINITE EYES  THE DREAM POWER  THE CIRCLING
  SKY  THE TREACHEROUS BIRDS  THE SHIFTING TOWNS  THE
  SNARLING GUNS  THE BURNING STORM  THE VAST RIVER  THE
 CLAY DANCERS  THE BLACK MASKS  THE RICH SANDS  THE HAZY
 DEMON  THE SCREAMING SKIES  THE VULTURES MOUTHS  THE RAW
 EYES  THE THUNDEROUS SONG  THE SHIFTING TRACKS  THE VAST
 CIRCLE  THE RATTLING BIRDS  THE DUSTY TENTS  THE GUNS SNARL
THE STEAMING HORIZON  THE BONE FOREST  THE BURNING TOWNS  THE
SAND FLOWERS  THE TREACHEROUS INFINITE  THE BLACK TRACKED  THE
DANCERS SCREAM  THE MASKED GUNS  THE THUNDERS MOUTH  THE FOREST
TOWN  THE CLAY HUTS  THE STORMS POWER  THE DRUGGED RIVER  THE
 SHIFTING SONGS  THE SKYS EYE  THE RATTLING DREAM  THE SNARLING DUST  THE
  SANDS DEMONS  THE BURNING BIRDS  THE CIRCLING HAZE  THE RAW BONES  THE
   RICH TENTS  THE SCREAMING FLOWER  THE STEAMING CLAY  THE BLACK SAND
   THE MASKED       DANCE    THE TREACHEROUS HORIZON  THE STORMS TRACK
                 THE RIVER THUNDER  THE SHIFTY VULTURES  THE
                FORESTS POWER  THE RAW SKY  THE SCREAMING
               EYES  THE DREAM SONGS  THE DRUGGED HUTS
              THE HAZY TOWNS  THE BURNT CIRCLE  THE
              GUNS MOUTH  THE SNARLING BONES  THE
              INFINITE BIRDS  THE DUSTY FLOWERS
               THE STORMS MASK  THE THUNDERING
               DEMONS  THE TENT DANCERS  THE
               RICH CLAY  THE SHIFTED POWER
               THE SANDY RIVER  THE BURNING
               TREACHERY  THE RATTLING TRACK
               THE BLACK STEAM  THE POWERFULL
               DREAM  THE FLOWERING SONG THE
               DRUGGED SCREAM  THE DANCING EYE          THE
               HORIZONAL HUT  THE MOUTHLESS           SNARLS
                THE TRACKLESS SKY  THE RAW          FOREST
                THE TENT TOWN  THE HAZY           RIVER
                THE INFINITE SHIFT  THE           BIRD
                 STORM  THE TREACHEROUS          DEMON
                 THE BURNING DRUG THE           GUN
                 DANCE  THE SINGING
                  BONE  THE MASKED
                  RICH  THE BLACK
                  CIRCLING  THE
                   VAST DREAM
                   SINGING
```

Dave Calder

Downhill Racer

Down
    the
        snow–
            white
        page
  we
slide.
    From
        side
          to
            side
          we
      glide.
         Pass
            obstacles
               with
                  ease.
               Words
           on
          skis.
      Look out.
            Here
        comes
    a
  poem
    in
      a
          hurry!

Uphill Climb

Wheeeeee

Three

Two

One

go.

another

have

to

top

the

to

back

way

the

all

climb

the

is

part

boring

only

The

Roger McGough

The Anaconda

The anaconda stretches a long long long long way - Its head is in tomorrow, while its tail's still in today

Richard Edwards

A Time for Roses

Illustrations by Lorraine Gum

ISBN: 1 86476 117 2

This edition for
SELECT EDITIONS
Devizes
Wiltshire, UK

A Time for
Roses

*Our highest assurance of the
goodness of providence seems to me
to rest in the flowers.
All other things, our desires, our food,
are really necessary for our existence
in the first instance.
But this rose is an extra. Its smell
and its colour are an embellishment
of life, not a
condition of it. It is only goodness
which gives extras, and so I say
again that we have much to hope for
from the flowers.*

Sir Arthur Conan Doyle
1859-1930

Oh whence could such a plant
have sprung?
The earth produced an infant flower.
Which springs with blushing
tinctures drest,
The gods beheld this brilliant earth.
And hailed the rose,
the boon on earth.

Anacreon
C.570-C.475 B.C.

This world that we're livin' in
Is mighty hard to beat;
You git a thorn with every Rose
But ain't the Roses sweet.

Frank L. Stanton

Loveliest of lovely things are they.
On earth that soonest pass away,
The rose that lives its little hour,
Is prized beyond the sculptured
flower.

William Cullen

Who ever called a rose a rose
Aptly named it, as it grows
So lovely with Its colours rare,
Its sweet perfume which fills the air.
'A rose by any other name'
they say –
I close my eyes, but come what may
No other name comes to my mind,
Because I know I'll only find
A rose can only be a Rose.

B.M.M.

Far-off, most secret and inviolate Rose,
Enfold me in my hour of hours.

W.B. Yeats 1865-1939

But never yet, by night or day,
In dew of spring, or summer's ray,
Did the sweet Valley shine so gay
As now it shines, all love and light,
Visions by day, and feasts by night!
A happier smile illumes each brow,
With quicker spread each heart
uncloses,
And all is ecstasy, - for now
The Valley holds its Feast of Roses.

Moore

The red rose whispers of passion
And the white rose breathes of love;
O, the red rose is a falcon,
And the white rose it a dove.

J.B. O'Reilly

One comes back
to those old-fashioned roses as
One does to old music
and poetry.
A garden needs old association,
old fragrances,
as a home needs things
that have been lived with.

From
"The Rose Annual", 1928

Real roses tumble, their petals upon
piano tops and carpets.
They have thorns and too many
leaves and smell of summer gardens.
They come with kisses.

Clara Oertega

I like old roses best.
Untidy, tousled, simple,
heavy-scented, thorned.
Comfortable company
on a drowsing summer's day.

Marion Garretty

I am the Rose of Sharon,
and the lily of the valley.
As the lily among thorns,
so is My love among the daughters.

Song of Solomon 2:12

A sepal, petal and thorn
Upon a common summers morn
A flash of dew – a bee or two –
A breeze – a caper in the trees –
And I'm a rose!

Emily Dickinson
1830–1886

I wonder,
I wonder if anyone knows,
Who lives in the heart of this velvety
rose, Now is it a goblin, or is it an elf,
Or is it the queen of the fairies herself.
Some prefer the Tea Rose
And some the Floribunda
Others choose the miniature
Over which to muse and wonder,
If the rambler, shrub, or climber,
Is best of all the roses.
But does it really matter
When guided by our noses.

Joe Shorthand

And I will make thee beds of roses,
And a thousand fragrant posies.

Christopher Marlowe
1564-1593

*There is no healing coolness
like that of the petals of a rose.*

Charlotte Gray

A rose is so unnecessarily beautiful.

Pam Brown

*I have this sense
that if the rose were to vanish,
there would be no more
beautiful summer days.*

Marion Garretty

Each rose that comes bring me greetings from the Rose of an eternal spring.

Rabindranath Tagore
1861-1941

*One lone rose in a sea of
waste and war,
out-blooms a feast of
common flowers showing
their finest faces in Heaven.*

T.P. Carolat

Flowers are the sweetest things that
God ever made
and forgot to put a soul into.

Henry Ward Beecher

What a pity flowers can utter
no sound?
A singing rose,
a whispering violet,
a murmuring honeysuckle, -
oh, what a rare and exquisite miracle
would these be!

Henry Ward Beecher

But as some lone wood-wandering
child
Brings home with him at evening
mild
The thorns and flowers of all the wild,
From your whole life
O fair and true,
Your flowers and thorns
you bring with you!

Robert Louis Stevenson

Fame is the scentless sunflower,
with gaudy crown of gold;
But friendship is
the breathing rose,
with sweets in every fold.

Oliver Wendell Holmes

They grow among desolation.
They shroud the scars of war.
They grant a haven to the desolate.
They bring hope to those who are
injured or ill.
They comfort the bereaved.
They mark remembrance.
They cheer city yard and
suburban garden.
They defy the machine.
They are lights in darkness.
They are the promise of renewal.
They are life.

Pam Brown

We live among marvels…each flower a masterpiece of subtle beauty, form and scent.

Marion Garretty

Gather therefore the rose,
whilst yet is prime.
For soon comes age,
that will her pride deflower.

Edmund Spenser

Go, lovely rose!
Tell her, that
wastes her time and me,
That now she knows,
When I resemble her to thee,
How sweet and fair she seems to be.
'Go, lovely rose!'

Edmund Waller

I have heard the mavis singing
Its love-song to the morn;
I've seen the dew-drop clinging
To the rose just newly born.

Charles Jefferys
1807 - 1865

Look to the Rose that blows
about us – 'Lo,
Laughing,' she says, 'into the
World I blow:
At once the silken tassel of
my purse
Tear, and it's treasure on the
Garden throw.'

God loved flowers
and created soil.
Man loved flowers
and created the vase.

It was a bowl of roses:
There in the light they lay,
Languishing, glorying, glowing
Their life away.
And the soul of them rose like
a presence,
Into me crept and grew,
And filled me with something
—some one
O, was it you?

William Ernest Henley
1849 - 1903

*How rare and wonderful is that
precious moment when we suddenly
and unexpectedly come upon
a perfect rose.*

T.P. Carolat

The Rose

I came upon a flower
So sweet, so pure
Its beauty so exquisite
It filled my heart with joy,
Enthralled I stood and gazed
I could not pass it by
Perfection such as this
Deserved more than a glance.
Its petals shone with dew
Like tears about to fall,
Oh Queen of all the flowers
It was a lovely rose.

Dorothy Lockett

My solace I find in my roses,
Their perfection of colour and form,
Their fragrant appeal and their
beauty,
Make one's outlook more peaceful
And warm.

Then in that party, all those powers
voted the rose The queen of flowers

Robert Herrick

The white-thorn, lovely May,
Opens her many lovely eyes
listening; the Rose still sleeps,
None dare to wake her; soon she
bursts her crimson-curtain'd bed
And comes forth in the majesty
of beauty.

William Blake
1757-1827

*Friendship is the finest rose in
the garden of life.*

...There should be beds of Roses,
banks of Roses, bowers of Roses,
hedges of Roses, edgings of Roses,
pillars of Roses, arches of Roses,
fountains of Roses, baskets of Roses,
vistas and alleys of the Rose.
Now overhead and now at our feet,
there they should creep and climb.
New tints, new forms, new perfumes,
should meet us at every turn.

S. Reynolds Hole

You love the roses –
so do I.
I wish The sky would rain
down roses,
as they rain from off the shaken
bush. Why will it not?
Then all the valley would be
pink and white
And soft to tread on.
They would fall as light as feathers,
smelling sweet; and it would be like
sleeping and yet waking, all at once.

George Eliot

People from a planet without flowers
would think we must be mad with
joy the whole time to have such
things about us.

Iris Murdock

*Don't complain
that your roses have thorns
Just be grateful
that your thorns have Roses.*

The price of a rose
is in a catalogue,
but the value of the rose
Is in one's heart.

What's in a name?
That which we call a rose
By any other name would smell as
sweet.
Sweet spring, full of sweet days and
roses
A box where sweets compacted lie.

You may break,
you may shatter the vase,
if you will,
But the scent of the roses
will hang round it still.

Thomas Moore
1779 – 1852

Tis the last rose of summer
Left blooming alone;
All her lovely companions
Are faded and gone.

Thomas Moore
1779 – 1852

He that plants thorns
must never expect to gather roses.

John Barlett
1820 – 1905

I remember I remember
The roses red and white
Those flowers made of light.

Thomas Hood

Summer perfected is a drowse of bees and roses.

Helen Thompson,
b.1943

The rainbow comes and goes
And lovely is the rose.

Elizabeth Wordsworth
1840 - 1932

Gather ye rosebuds while ye may,
Old Time is still a-flying:
And this same flower that smiles today
Tomorrow will be dying.

Robert Herrick
1591 – 1674

The seasons alter, hoary-headed frosts
Fall in the fresh lap of the crimson rose.

William Shakespeare